efore

TD4754

Religion

Tony D. Triggs

Wayland

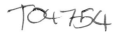

Titles in the series

Cover illustrations: *Background* Title page of John Foxe's Book of Martyrs. *Inset* Cardinal Wolsey.

First published in 1993 by Wayland (Publishers) Ltd
61 Western Road, Hove, East Sussex BN3 1JD

Editor: Cath Senker
Designer: John Christopher
Consultant: Linda Goddard, Primary History Advisory Teacher, Runnymede Staff Development Centre, Surrey

British Library Cataloguing in Publication Data

Triggs, Tony D.
  Religion. – (Tudors and Stuarts series)
  I. Title II. Series
  274.1

ISBN 0-7502-0763-9

Typeset by Strong Silent Type
Printed and bound by B.P.C.C. Paulton Books, Great Britain

Picture acknowledgements
Ashmolean Museum 19 (right), 21 (both); Bede Monastery Museum 6 (Copyright Biblioteca Medicea Laurenziana, Florence); Bridgeman Art Library 8; British Film Institute 9 (below); British Museum 5,18; Camera Press 26 (both); Chapel Studios 27 (above); Ann Dean of Malvern 13; ET Archives 25; Historic Scotland (British Museum) 7; Michael Holford 4; Hulton Picture Library 10; Mansell Collection *cover* (background),15, 19 (left); National Maritime Museum 16,17; National Portrait Gallery *cover* (inset), title page,12,14, 20; National Trust 22 (above),23; Skyscan 9 (above); Topham 27 (below); Victoria and Albert Museum 24; Wayland Picture Library 11 (British Museum), 22 (below).

Notes for teachers

Religion includes a wide range of exciting sources including contemporary artefacts, paintings and drawings. This book:

◆ helps the reader to understand the complex religious changes of Tudor and Stuart times, and explains why religion was so central to people's lives.

◆ Provokes discussion of historical bias by giving different views for the reader to consider.

◆ Shows how the religious changes of the period helped to shape Christian religious practices in Britain today.

Contents

The power of the Church

The Tudor kings and queens ruled England and Wales from 1485 to 1603, and the Stuarts ruled England, Scotland and Wales from 1603 to 1714. In those days the Christian religion was very important in people's lives. Most people went to church on Sunday, and also at special times of the year, like Christmas.

Going to church

There was no excuse for Tudor people to arrive late for church. Most churches had a tower with a bell, and someone rang it to call people from their fields and cottages. If anyone stayed away from church, a special church court would make that person pay a fine.

This fourteenth century church was used in Tudor times.

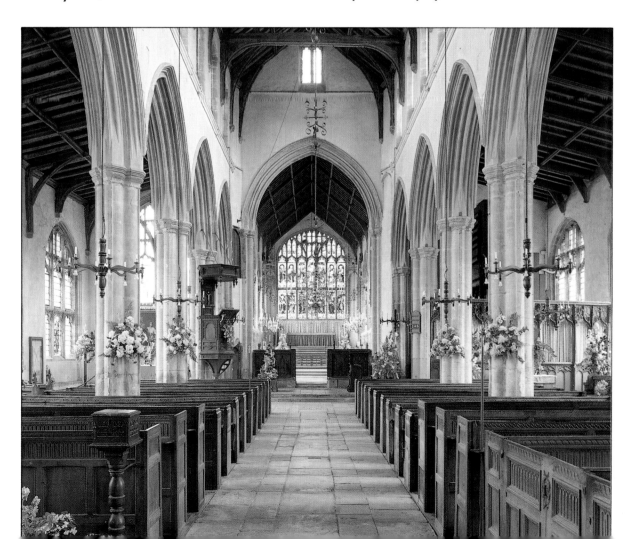

People were used to the church services, but they probably felt uncomfortable and bored at times. They had to sit on hard wooden seats, or on the cold stone floor. The services went on for hours, and most of the words were in Latin, a language few people could understand.

Working for the Church

The Christian Church employed many workers. Some were needed to build new churches. They had to cut tree-trunks or slabs of stone to make building blocks. Then, as the church grew taller, they had to lift the wood or stone using a hoist (a sort of crane). Some of them died in accidents, but without the wages they earned for the work, they would have starved.

Workers in the late fifteenth century building a tower.

The Church owned large amounts of land with many farms. Some people worked on them as shepherds and ploughmen. Other people had their own crops and animals, but the Church often owned the land they used and the cottages in which they lived. They had to pay rent, and this helped to make the Church very rich. They also had to give the Church a share of their crops. Some of the barns where they stored the crops can still be seen today.

Monasteries

Monasteries were buildings where men (called monks) devoted their lives to the Christian religion. They had to say prayers several times a day, and also at night. Women (called nuns) lived similar lives in buildings called convents. There were about 700 monasteries and convents in Britain in 1500.

A monk copying out a book.

Copying books

Henry VII was the first Tudor king. When he came to the throne in 1485 there were hardly any books, and very few people could read or write. Ways of printing books were being improved at that time, but most books were still copied out by hand. Monks could read and write so they did most of the copying work.

The Church banned books with new ideas about religion or science. Monks and nuns were only allowed to read and copy books which contained the old ideas which the Church had taught for hundreds of years.

A modern artist's idea of **Melrose Abbey**, Scotland, in Tudor times.

Monastery buildings

Henry VIII, who reigned from 1509 to 1547, sometimes went to pray at the monastery in Walsingham, Norfolk. It took three days to get there from London on horseback. Henry made the journey because Walsingham was a holy place for Christians. Today the journey to Walsingham would take only two or three hours by car.

Melrose Abbey was a monastery like the one at Walsingham. In the picture above, an artist has drawn it as it would have looked in Tudor times. The building with the tower was the church where the monks used to pray. The monks lived and worked in the other buildings. What else can you learn about their way of life from the picture?

Henry VIII and the Church in England and Wales

The Church was ruled by a man called the Pope, who lived in Rome. The Pope expected people – even kings – to obey him. Henry VIII began to disobey the Pope, and he started to rule the Church in England and Wales himself.

A portrait of Henry VIII.

Henry's divorce

Henry's trouble with the Church began when he wanted to divorce his first wife, Catherine of Aragon. In those days, the Church and Pope decided whether people could have divorces or not. In Henry's case the Pope refused, so in 1535 Henry made himself the Head of the Church in England, instead of the Pope. That meant that there was no one to stop him divorcing Catherine and marrying again. His second wife was called Anne Boleyn.

Henry and the monasteries

As head of the Church, Henry closed down the monasteries and sent the monks and nuns away. This was partly because he needed the monasteries' money and land to pay for foreign wars.

Some of the empty monasteries fell down because there was no one looking after them, and builders pulled some of them down to get the wood and stone. You can still see some of the ruined monasteries. There are monks and nuns in Britain today, but their monasteries were started after the time of Henry VIII.

A man called Cardinal Wolsey helped Henry to close the monasteries. The picture below comes from a film called *A Man for All Seasons*. What is the actor trying to show you about Wolsey?

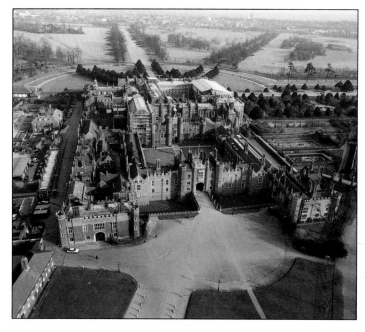

Hampton Court Palace.

We can check things in films by studying clues from long ago. Wolsey's magnificent home, called Hampton Court Palace, shows that Wolsey grew very rich through helping to close the monasteries.

The actor who played Cardinal Wolsey in *A Man for All Seasons*.

Changes in religion

By about 1525 printed books were becoming common. Few people could read, but those who could do so began to get copies of the Bible and other printed books. Some of the things they read surprised them. They started to question the Church and its ideas about the world and religion.

Books and ideas

The Church taught that the Sun moves round the Earth, but some scientists said that the Earth moves round the Sun. The Church tried to stop them saying this, but the new printed books helped to spread the scientists' ideas.

A printer's workshop.

Complaints and protests

Scholars and others began to complain about the Church's greed, and they said that church services were too mysterious. They did not like the priests' fine robes, and the fact that they stood at a fancy altar chanting in Latin. They also said that the Church was wrong when it claimed that all its teachings and actions were based on the Bible. People who agreed with these protests (complaints) were called Protestants.

The Bible had always been written in Latin. Protestants wanted people to read it for themselves, so Protestant scholars turned it into English and other common languages.

This page comes from one of the first printed Bibles. What language is it in?

Protestants and Roman Catholics

Henry VIII died in 1547 and his son became King Edward VI. He also took over as Head of the Church in England and Wales. Protestant ideas now spread quickly and priests made their services simpler and easier to understand. English was used instead of Latin and tables were used instead of altars. Similar changes were happening in much of northern Europe.

A portrait of Edward VI.

Roman Catholics

Some people in England and Wales refused to change their ideas and their ways of praying. They continued to obey the Pope, and they said that kings who tried to take his place were acting wickedly. These people were known as Roman Catholics.

Many English people were afraid that Catholics in southern Europe would one day go to war against England. This made them very suspicious of the Catholics they knew. They thought they might be spying for other countries. They also thought they might try to kill the king and replace him with a Catholic king.

Here is a priest-hole where a Catholic priest used to hide.

1509
Henry VIII
becomes king.

About 1535
The first printed
Bibles begin to
appear in
England.

1535
Henry makes
himself Head of
the Church in
England.

1539
Henry begins
closing the
monasteries.

1547
Henry dies.
Edward VI
becomes King
and Head of the
Church.

A priest-hole

The churches in England and Wales were used by Protestants, so Roman Catholics no longer had churches to use for their services. Instead, they had to pray at home. Rich Roman Catholic families had their own priests and altars. Having a Roman Catholic priest in your home was against the law, so priests had to hide in secret rooms. These hiding places were sometimes called priest-holes.

Queen Mary

Edward died as a teenager, and Henry VIII's eldest daughter Mary Tudor became queen. Mary was a Roman Catholic, and she tried to make England a Roman Catholic country again. She put many Protestant leaders to death. Altars were brought back into churches, and services were held in Latin again.

A portrait of Queen Mary.

What was Mary like?

We can learn many things from paintings, but we have to use them carefully. For example, artists usually missed out people's spots and scars and they often tried to show what they thought of the person.

Look carefully at the portrait of Mary. Do you think the artist liked her – or not?

Foxe's *Book of Martyrs*

Shortly after Mary's death, a man called John Foxe wrote a book called the *Book of Martyrs*. Martyrs are people who would rather die than change their religion.

This picture comes from Foxe's book. On the left of the picture we see some of the Protestants who were put to death during Mary's reign. They are dying bravely and going to heaven. On the right we see what the artist thought of Roman Catholics.

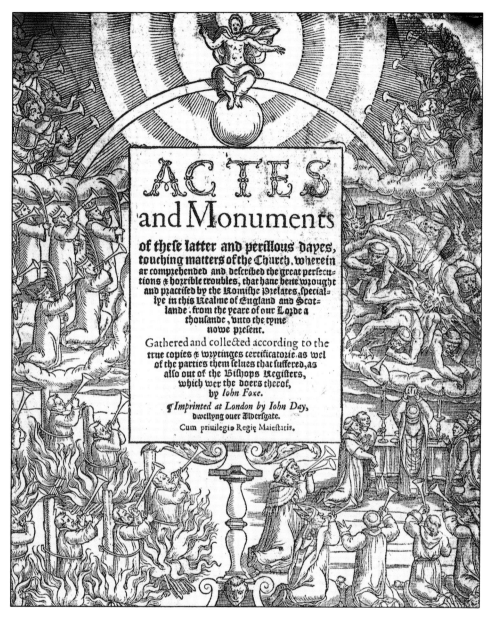

A picture from Foxe's *Book of Martyrs*. **How do you think it affected people's thoughts and feelings?**

Elizabeth I became queen after Mary. She was a Protestant, so she became the head of the Church in England and Wales. She brought back Protestant ways of praying, but she let Roman Catholics pray as they wanted in their homes.

The Spanish Armada

Spain was a Roman Catholic country. Encouraged by the Pope, its king decided to conquer England and make it a Catholic country again. In 1588 a Spanish fleet, the Armada, set sail.

Ships of the Spanish Armada near the English coast.

Praying for victory

Some of the Spanish ships had holy flags. The Spaniards knew that the Pope and the Roman Catholic Church were on their side. They felt that God was on their side too. They said special prayers before they sailed, and their flags reminded them to pray every day.

Stopped by a gale

The Spaniards' plans went badly wrong. The English used burning ships to set some of the Spanish ships on fire. Then a gale blew the Spanish ships off course and some were wrecked on the Scottish coast. Other ships got home to Spain but the Spaniards did not attack England again.

The English had prayed as much as the Spaniards, and they felt that God had sent the gale to help them. After the gale, they showed how pleased and grateful they were by making medals like the one in the photograph. The words round the edge say 'God breathed and they [the Spaniards] were scattered'.

1553-8
Queen Mary's reign. Protestant leaders are put to death.

1558
Queen Elizabeth comes to the throne.

1588
The Spanish Armada is defeated.

A medal made in England after the danger was over.

17

The Church under James I and VI

Scotland had a king called James VI. When Elizabeth died without children, James became king of England too. The English call him James I. He was the first Stuart king of England, and he was followed by his son, Charles I.

James was a Protestant. Some Roman Catholics did not think that he had the right to rule. A group of them decided to kill him. They rented a cellar underneath the Houses of Parliament and filled it with gunpowder. They planned to set the gunpowder off on 5 November 1605, when James was due to be in the building.

The Gunpowder Plot failed. Protestants felt that God had been laughing at the plotters while they worked. They made drawings with the Latin words *Video Rideo* – I see and I laugh. The words were supposed to be coming from God.

The Gunpowder Plotters.

Charles' supporters wrote books about the Divine Right of Kings. The page below comes from one of these books. The man on the right is a king, and an angel is holding a Bible for him to read. The artist is saying that God likes kings, and that kings obey God. The man on the left is pulling out his sword, because he does not want to have a king.

The first page of the New Testament (part of the Bible) in Welsh. It was printed during James' reign. James also had a new translation of the Bible printed in English. It is called the King James Bible.

Pictures and books

James and Charles both stuck to a very old idea – that God gives kings and queens the right to rule as they wish. This is called the Divine (or God-given) Right of Kings.

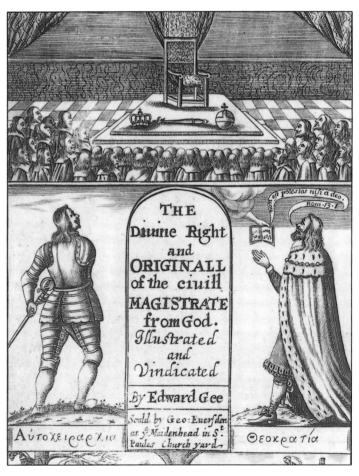

This picture is by an artist who believed that kings should rule as they liked.

The English Civil War and the Puritans

The idea that kings can rule as they like led to trouble in Charles' reign. Parliament disagreed with Charles about taxes, but Charles and his friends felt that Parliament had no right to argue or interfere. In 1642 a war broke out between people who supported Charles and people who supported Parliament. It is usually called the Civil War.

A portrait of Oliver Cromwell. What sort of person does he seem to be?

Cromwell and the Puritans

Parliament's forces were led by a soldier called Oliver Cromwell. Cromwell had fought in Ireland, where most of the people were Catholics. Protestant landlords from England had taken much of their land, and the Irish had risen up against their English landlords. Cromwell had defeated the rebels and treated them very harshly.

Cromwell and most of his supporters were Puritans. Puritans were Protestants who believed in living and praying as simply as possible. They wore plain clothes and avoided fun and entertainment.

Hatred of Catholics

During the Civil War, Puritans and other strict Protestants felt very angry towards Catholics. They burned many Catholic books and ornaments. Can you see what they are burning in the picture? (You could read the writing to find out.)

These soldiers on Parliament's side are burning things that remind them of Roman Catholics.

Destroying altars

Some Protestant churches had ornaments and altars just like the ones which Catholics used. Puritan soldiers sometimes broke into churches and destroyed all the fine things they could find.

What are these soldiers doing in the church?

Life and religion under Cromwell

Parliament, led by Cromwell, won the Civil War. Charles was put in prison, and in 1649 his head was cut off. Cromwell began to rule in his place – though he called himself Lord Protector, not King. He and his Puritan followers closed down the theatres and inns, and they stopped people having parties and fun.

The church at Staunton Harold, built in 1653.

A Puritan preacher and two priests.

There are many drawings of Puritans, showing what different people thought of them. Some drawings poked fun at them, but others made them look wise and respectable. This drawing (left) shows a Puritan preacher and two priests. Perhaps you can work out what the artist thought of the Puritans. Some people felt that Puritan preachers shouted too much and attracted rather badly-behaved crowds.

A lesson in stone

This church (left) was built by someone who disagreed with the Puritans. Instead of making the building plain, he made it as fine and grand as he could. He explained his ideas on a stone fixed over one of the doors. See how much of it you can read.

The builder of the church at Staunton Harold explained here why he had built a fancy church, not a plain one.

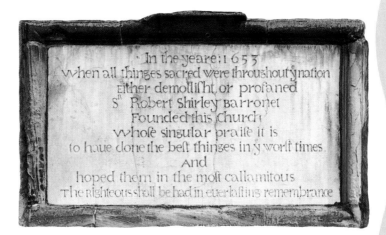

In the yeare: 1653
when all things sacred were throughout ỹ nation
Either demollisht, or profaned
Sʳ Robert Shirley Barronet
Founded this Church
whose singular praise it is
to haue done the best things in ỹ worst times
And
hoped them in the most callamitous
The righteous shall be had in euerlasting remembrance

The Vicar of Bray

Some clergymen stuck to what they believed in, although it meant risking their jobs or their lives. Others changed with the times. They removed their altars or put them back to suit the latest ruler. The Vicar of Bray, who lived in Berkshire, was one of the men who did this. People still remember him in a song. According to the song, he said to the people in his church:

> " *Whatsoever king shall reign*
> *I'll still be the Vicar of Bray.* "

Maybe you could find out the rest of the words.

The conflict in Ireland

Cromwell ruled until his death in 1658.
By that time people were tired of the
Puritans' harshness, and in 1660
Parliament asked Charles' elder son to
become King Charles II. He was
followed by his brother James II, who
came to the throne in 1685.

Some people felt that Charles I had died in
a brave and holy way, just like a martyr.
They showed Charles I and Charles II in
pictures like the one below. What were they
saying about Charles II, the man on the left?

A painting of the Battle of the Boyne in 1690.

The Battle of the Boyne

James II was a Roman Catholic, and this helped to make him very unpopular. In the end he was driven out of England, and his Protestant daughter Mary and her Dutch husband William took his place.

In 1690 James went to Ireland. He raised an army to fight against William and Mary. The Irish were glad to help him because they hated their Protestant landlords from England, and they still remembered Cromwell's cruelty.

However, William and Mary's troops defeated James' troops at the Battle of the Boyne. William punished the Irish Catholics who had supported James. He took away their land and gave it to his English friends.

You can see why the Irish people became angry with the English. What do you think it was like to be a Protestant settler in Ireland in such troubled times?

From past to present

Things that happened in Tudor and Stuart times affect people's lives today. There is unrest and bitterness in Northern Ireland because of the way the English and Scottish Protestants treated the Irish Catholics. Protestants and Catholics still get on badly there.

These Protestants in Northern Ireland march every year to celebrate the Battle of the Boyne. How do you think Catholics feel about this march?

National churches

England and Scotland have churches belonging to the Church of England and the Church of Scotland. The Queen is head of the Church of England. This goes back to the time of Henry VIII and his quarrel with the Pope. In those days the Church had enormous power, and it still has some of that power today. For example, twenty-two Church of England bishops have a right to vote in the House of Lords.

Elizabeth II, the Queen Mother and Prince William leaving church.

Since Tudor and Stuart times, many people who are not Christians have come to live in Britain. The biggest group are Muslims, who pray in mosques.

The Church of England has kept its special place in the House of Lords, but it can no longer make people go to services. Nowadays, less than five people out of every hundred do so regularly. Some people go to other churches, including Roman Catholic ones, and others worship at mosques and temples. However, most people do not go to a place of worship at all.

History in our pockets
Look for the letters FD on this modern coin. They stand for the Latin words *Fidei Defensor* (Defender of the Faith). The Pope gave Henry VIII this title before they quarrelled and most English kings and queens have used it ever since.

A modern coin, showing Queen Elizabeth II.

People dressed in seventeenth century-style clothes at a Bonfire Night procession. Can you see the man dressed as the Pope?

Bonfire Night
One of the Roman Catholics who plotted to blow up Parliament on 5 November 1605 was called Guy Fawkes. Many people remember him every 5 November on Bonfire Night. They make model Guys to burn on their fires. In some parts of Britain people also remember the Protestant martyrs who died when Mary Tudor was Queen. Their angry processions show hatred for Roman Catholics.

Officials still search the cellars of Parliament every year to make sure there is not a new lot of gunpowder there!

Timeline

1480	1500	1520	1540	1560	1580

Tudors

1485 HENRY VII

1509 HENRY VIII

1547 EDWARD VI

1553 MARY TUDOR

1558 ELIZABETH I

1480–1500	1500–1520	1520–1540	1540–1560	1560–1580	1580–1600
1492 Columbus sails to America.	**1500–1547** Sheep farmers enclose common land. **1509** Cabot tries to sail round the north of Canada. **1511** The *Great Michael* is launched.	**1520** The Spaniards start to colonize the American mainland. **1535** Henry VIII becomes Head of the Church in England and Wales. **1536** Anne Boleyn is put to death. **1539** Henry VIII has the monasteries destroyed.	**1543** Vesalius publishes his book about the human body. **1545** The *Mary Rose* sinks. **1547–1553** Protestants are persecuted and put to death. **1547–1553** Many schools and colleges are built. **1549** Robert Kett leads a rebellion in Norfolk.	**1560s** Drake makes merchant voyages with John and William Hawkins. **1567** As a Catholic, Mary Queen of Scots flees from Scotland but is imprisoned in England. **1577** Drake sets off on his voyage around the world.	**1587** Mary Queen of Scots is executed. **1588** The Spanish Armada is defeated. **1595** Raleigh explores South America. **1590–1616** Shakespeare writes his plays.

1600   1620   1640   1660   1680   1700

Stuarts

1603 JAMES I (JAMES VI OF SCOTLAND)

1625 CHARLES I

1649–1660 COMMONWEALTH
1653 OLIVER CROMWELL
1658 RICHARD CROMWELL
1660 CHARLES II

1685 JAMES II
1688 WILLIAM III & MARY II

1702–1714 ANNE

1600–1620

1605
The Gunpowder Plot.

1607
Henry Hudson sets off to explore the coast of northern Canada.

1610
Hudson discovers a huge bay in northern Canada that is named after him.

1620
The Pilgrim Fathers go to America.

1620–1640

1628
William Harvey describes how blood goes round the body.

1630–1641
Charles I rules without Parliament.

1640–1660

1642
The Civil War begins.

1646
Charles I is captured and imprisoned.

1649
Charles I is executed.

1649–1660
England and Wales are ruled without a king or queen.

1660–1680

1665
The Plague.

1666
The Great Fire of London.

1670
The Hudson Bay Company is founded.

1660–1669
Samuel Pepys writes his diary.

1660–1685
Hooke and Newton study light and gravitation.

Sir Christopher Wren designs many new buildings.

1670–1689
Aphra Behn writes her lively plays.

1680–1700

1690
The Battle of the Boyne.

1694
Queen Mary dies.

1680–1695
Henry Purcell writes his music.

1698
Scots set up Darien colony in South America, which fails.

1700–1710

1707
England and Scotland are officially united.

Glossary

Altar The fancy table which is used for religious services.

Banned Forbidden, not allowed.

Cardinal A very important man in the Roman Catholic Church, who advises the Pope.

Cellar A room underneath a building.

The Church The official Christian Church.

Divorce An official agreement to end a marriage.

Gunpowder A substance that explodes when set off by a gun or by fire.

Holy Specially connected with God.

Landlords People who own and rent out land or homes.

Medal A piece of metal shaped like a large coin, made to celebrate a special event.

Mysterious Strange.

Priests People whose job is to perform religious ceremonies.

Rebels People who fight against their rulers.

Robes Long, flowing clothes worn by priests.

Service A religious ceremony.

Books to read

Easy books

Anderson, D., *The Spanish Armada* (Macdonald, 1988)

Middleton, H., *Everyday Life in the Sixteenth Century* (Macdonald, 1982)

Triggs, T.D., *Tudor Britain* (Wayland, 1989)

Triggs, T.D., *Tudor and Stuart Times* (Folens, 1992)

Wood, T. *The Stuarts* (Ladybird, 1991)

Slide set

Tudor Background H. Baddeley Productions, 54 Moffats Lane, Brookmans Park, Hatfield, Herts AL9 7RU tel. 0707 54046

Books for older readers

Carter, M., Culpin and Kinloch, N. *Past into Present 2: 1400 – 1700* (Collins Educational, 1990)

Cooper, J. and Morris, S., *The Cromwell Family* (Thornes and Hulton, 1987)

Kelly, R. and T., *Oxford: A City at War* (Thornes and Hulton, 1987)

Kelly, T., *Children in Tudor England* (Thornes and Hulton, 1987)

Morris, R., *Bare Ruined Choirs: The Fate of a Welsh Abbey* (Thornes and Hulton, 1987)

Reische, D. *Founding the American Colonies* (Watts, 1989)

Places to visit

Churches:

Farndon, Cheshire – Church with windows showing Civil War troops

Staunton Harold, Leicestershire – Church with famous inscription

Palaces:

Hampton Court Palace, Richmond, London

Holyrood Palace, Edinburgh

Monasteries:

Bolton Abbey, North Yorkshire; Buildwas, Shropshire; Castle Acre, Norfolk; Kirkstall, West Yorkshire; Tintern, Gwent

Museums and exhibitions:

Cromwell's Museum, Huntingdon, Cambridgeshire

Index

Words in **bold** are subjects shown in pictures as well as in the text.